Original title:
A World Unknown

Copyright © 2024 Creative Arts Management OÜ
All rights reserved.

Author: Julian Carmichael
ISBN HARDBACK: 978-9916-90-568-5
ISBN PAPERBACK: 978-9916-90-569-2

Songs of the Unobserved

Whispers ride the evening breeze,
Hidden tales in rustling leaves.
Stars blink softly, secrets shared,
In shadows cast, dreams are bared.

Each note a story left unheard,
In silence forged, the heart is stirred.
Voices echo through the night,
In unseen realms, they take flight.

Spaces Beyond the Known

In realms where maps lose their way,
The colors dance, in bright array.
Curves of time and folds of light,
Reveal the magic of the night.

Each step unfolds a path untold,
In whispers sweet, the brave and bold.
Dimensions call with gentle grace,
To wander far from our own place.

The Pulse of Untold Stories

Deep within the stillness lie,
Echoes of a fleeting sigh.
Threads of fate intertwine and weave,
In hearts where unspent dreams believe.

Beneath the surface, life does hum,
With every beat, new tales become.
Rich with lore, our spirits yearn,
For every page, a twist and turn.

In the Hush of Twilight's Cloak

As day surrenders to the night,
Soft shadows gather, cloaked in light.
A quiet breath, the world in pause,
Nature sways, without a cause.

In twilight's grasp, the heart does find,
A gentle peace, so sweet and blind.
Time unravels in soft embrace,
In the hush, we find our place.

Footprints in Forgotten Sands

With each step, silence stays,
The waves, they whisper in soft plays.
A path unseen, the tide will claim,
Yet still I walk, know not the name.

In grains of gold, lost tales reside,
Echoes of dreams where shadows hide.
Each footprint marks a fleeting thought,
In lonely realms where hope is sought.

The Compass of Imagination

A needle spins, where visions flow,
Through realms of dreams, to worlds aglow.
Each thought a star in boundless night,
Guiding my heart to realms of light.

Maps drawn in hues of distant fire,
Carving paths of unquenched desire.
With every turn, new tales unfold,
As courage sparks the brave and bold.

Horizon of the Unseen

Beyond the mist, where shadows meet,
Lies a horizon, bittersweet.
A promise lingers, ever near,
Yet cloaked in dreams we hold so dear.

In twilight's embrace, secrets intertwine,
The heart's whisper, a call divine.
As stars awaken from slumber's kiss,
The unseen beckons, we seek the bliss.

Lanterns in the Darkened Unknown

In shadows thick, where fears reside,
A flicker glows, a guiding light.
Each lantern held with trembling hands,
A beacon bright in foreign lands.

Together we navigate the night,
With hearts aflame, we chase the fright.
In every corner, stories sneer,
Yet lanterns shimmer, drowned in fear.

Eclipsed Realities

In shadowed light, the stars align,
Whispers of fate weave through the night.
The moon is masked, a silent sign,
Dreams blend with the dark out of sight.

Time stands still in a breathless pause,
Hearts beat softly, a muted sound.
Reality bends, without a cause,
In the stillness, lost souls are found.

Shattered truths in a cosmic dance,
Echoes linger on the edge of thought.
Fleeting moments, a stolen glance,
Memories fade, but lessons are taught.

Beneath the Surface of Tomorrow

Waves of time crash on the shore,
Hidden depths hold secrets untold.
Each breath a quest, a longing for,
The spark of hope in dreams of gold.

Yet shadows lurk in the quiet tide,
Glimmers of doubt rise like the sun.
Beneath the echoes, fears we hide,
In the silence, we fight, we run.

Tomorrow waits with patient grace,
An open book, unwritten lines.
With every choice, we start the chase,
Beneath the waves, the light still shines.

Veils of Hidden Realities

Glimmers fade through curtains drawn,
Mysteries weave in a silent thread.
In the twilight, a world is born,
Whispers linger where few have tread.

Veils of fate obscure the truth,
Colors blend in a vivid haze.
Lost in the maze of eternal youth,
We seek the fire in ashen days.

But every shadow tells a tale,
Of dreams and fears forever bound.
Through the mist, we shall prevail,
In hidden realms, our hearts resound.

Echoes from the Unseen

Voices echo from realms unknown,
Notes of yearning fill the air.
Through the silence, seeds are sown,
A symphony of love and care.

Fragments dance in the moonlit glow,
Tales of journeys, paths embraced.
In empty spaces, we come to know,
The hidden dreams we once chased.

From shadows deep, stories arise,
Carried forth on a gentle breeze.
In the unseen, the spirit flies,
Boundless hearts, seeking their ease.

The Light of Unseen Stars

In velvet skies where shadows play,
A whisper of light begins to sway.
From distant realms they softly gleam,
Illuminating every dream.

They guide the lost through darkest nights,
With twinkling hopes and gentle sights.
Each flicker tells a story bold,
Of love, of life, of tales untold.

Unraveled Threads of Eternity

A tapestry of time unfurls,
Where moments dance like sea-salt pearls.
Each thread a choice, a path unmade,
In shadows deep, past games we've played.

Yet through the mist, the colors shine,
In intricate patterns, they entwine.
Our stories woven, rich and vast,
In every thread, a piece of past.

Reflections in a Glass of Mystery

A crystal orb that holds the night,
With secrets locked from human sight.
It spins and sways with every breath,
In silent whispers, it teases death.

What visions lie beyond the glass?
What futures wait as shadows pass?
In mirrored depths, the heart can see,
The echoes of what's yet to be.

Poems from the Edge of Dusk

As daylight fades to twilight's bloom,
We weave our words in evening's room.
The sky ignites in hues of fire,
In every shade, a soul's desire.

With murmurs soft as evening dew,
We capture dreams, both old and new.
These fleeting thoughts on air we cast,
A serenade for shadows past.

The Other Side of Silence

Whispers linger in the air,
Secrets hidden everywhere.
In the hush, a heart can plead,
Yearning for what it might need.

In the stillness, shadows dance,
Dreams awaken, take their chance.
Words unspoken, feelings swell,
In the silence, truths can dwell.

Echoes soft as twilight fades,
Memory in twilight shades.
Hearts entwined in silent thread,
Voices hushed, yet widely spread.

Crossing over to the light,
Breaking through the endless night.
On the other side, we find,
Peaceful echoes left behind.

Traverse the Unfathomed

Through the fog, our journey calls,
Into depths where silence falls.
Paths uncharted lay ahead,
Where the unknown leaves us led.

Each step taken, fears reside,
But with courage, we will glide.
Stars above our guiding light,
As we traverse the endless night.

Whispers of the ocean's song,
In the depths where we belong.
Every wave a story told,
In the unfathomed, hearts grow bold.

With each heartbeat, we shall roam,
Finding in the dark a home.
Beyond the edge where shadows play,
We shall find our bright new day.

Echoes from Distant Horizons

Over valleys, beyond the hills,
Every breeze a memory thrills.
In the distance, voices sigh,
Softly calling from the sky.

Footsteps tread on ancient ground,
In the silence, echoes found.
Every shadow holds a tale,
In the dusk where dreams unveil.

Chasing light through shifting sands,
Grains of time slip through our hands.
Horizons stretch like painted skies,
In their beauty, hope will rise.

Echoes of the past will guide,
In their warmth, we will abide.
From the distance, futures sing,
In the echoes, life takes wing.

In the Depth of Shadowed Dreams

In the night where shadows creep,
Lies a world that's ours to keep.
Whispers wrapped in velvet seams,
Dance within our shadowed dreams.

Colors blur with silent sighs,
Tragic beauty never dies.
In the dark, our spirits soar,
Seeking what we yearn for more.

Visions weave a tangled thread,
Chasing thoughts that dance ahead.
Through the depths, we find our way,
Guided by the stars' soft sway.

Awake or lost in endless night,
Every dream ignites the light.
In the depth of what remains,
Hope is found where love obtains.

Beyond the Familiar Facade

Behind the smile, shadows play,
Whispers of dreams fade away.
Masks we wear, secrets kept,
In lonely nights, truths adept.

Colors blend, yet pale they seem,
Life moves on—a fleeting dream.
Upon the walls, echoes bounce,
In silence, lost hopes renounce.

Beneath the laughter, pain resides,
A silent storm, where joy hides.
Yet still we rise, we wear our guise,
To face the world with coded ties.

Elixirs of Uncertainty

In shadows cast, decisions loom,
Heartbeats quicken, fate finds room.
Sips of courage, doubts entwine,
Sip the poison, sweet the brine.

Paths ahead, shrouded in mist,
Choices made, none can resist.
With every step, risks intertwine,
Elixirs of life, endlessly divine.

Yet hope remains, a flicker bright,
Guiding souls through endless night.
To navigate the winding way,
In uncertainty, we learn to stay.

Visions from the Hidden

In whispers soft, the secrets flow,
Beneath the surface, worlds aglow.
Glimmers of truth in shadows play,
Visions beckon, lead astray.

Windows closed, yet hearts aflame,
What lies beyond? Who's to blame?
In darkened rooms, we seek the light,
To pierce through veils and take our flight.

The hidden paths, where few have tread,
Woven dreams, the words unsaid.
With eyes wide open, we unveil,
The stories buried, where souls sail.

The Silence of Untrodden Grounds

In quiet places, thoughts collide,
A tranquil space where fears abide.
Beneath the trees, the stillness speaks,
In gentle whispers, nature seeks.

With every footstep, echoes pause,
Amidst the beauty, there's no cause.
Untrodden paths, where shadows weave,
In silence lies what we believe.

The air is thick with tales untold,
In every moment, life unfolds.
To tread where few have dared to roam,
In silence, we discover home.

Constellations of Hidden Truth

In the night sky, secrets glow,
Stars whisper tales of long ago.
Each twinkle holds a mystic rhyme,
Guiding souls through space and time.

Beneath the velvet, shadows play,
Illuminating dreams that stray.
Through cosmic paths, we boldly tread,
Searching for light where we once led.

Galaxies bloom in silent grace,
Embedding wisdom in their space.
In the vastness, we are but dust,
Yet boundless truths, we still must trust.

Constellation maps, we chart our quest,
In the darkness, we find our rest.
Through hidden truths, our spirits soar,
In the wonder, we crave for more.

The Tapestry of the Unperceived

Threads of silence weave the night,
In the shadows, shapes take flight.
Colorless hues, yet deep they flow,
Stories of worlds we do not know.

Fleeting moments stitch our dreams,
Captured whispers, like delicate beams.
In every knot, life intertwines,
The unseen hand, where fate aligns.

In a fabric worn, the past enfold,
History's secrets, gently told.
A tapestry rich with echoes found,
In the unperceived, life's threads abound.

Lines of existence twist and bend,
In the unseen, we seek to mend.
Through intricate patterns, hearts will weave,
In each connection, we learn to believe.

Whispers of the Without

Gentle breezes carry the sound,
Of life outside, where dreams abound.
Nature sings in quiet tones,
In every leaf, a voice intones.

Cascading whispers, like a sigh,
Echoing truths that never die.
Through rustling branches, secrets flee,
A symphony of serenity.

Mountains stand in stoic grace,
Guarding thoughts in their embrace.
With every rustle, the world unveils,
The softest heart where silence prevails.

Within the vastness, we find our place,
In whispers heard, we trace our grace.
Connecting worlds, both near and far,
In the without, we find who we are.

Driftwood from Other Shores

Washed ashore from distant lands,
Stories held in weathered strands.
Each piece of wood, a journey's trace,
Whispers of time and ancient grace.

Carved by waves, shaped by the tide,
Lessons of life in every stride.
Nature's art, both wild and free,
Driftwood tells of what can be.

Fragments of homes long since gone,
Echoes of laughter linger on.
In their grain, the sun's embrace,
Silent comfort, a warm embrace.

Collected dreams on sandy shores,
In driftwood's heart, the ocean roars.
From shores unseen, wisdom flows,
In every line, a tale bestows.

Skylines of the Forgotten

Beneath the shadows, old towers rise,
Whispers of settings beneath dark skies.
Echoes of laughter in the fading light,
Memories linger, lost in the night.

Faded murals, tales etched in stone,
Ghosts of the past, never alone.
The wind carries secrets, soft and slight,
Calling the dreamers to take their flight.

Broken windows, frames of despair,
Silent streets echo the longing air.
Time moves slowly, yet we remain,
Yearning for moments that slip like rain.

Above the rooftops, lonely birds soar,
Searching for comfort, forevermore.
In these skylines, the forgotten dwell,
In every heartbeat, a story to tell.

Treading on Invisible Paths

In the forest's embrace, we tread so light,
Crushed leaves whisper secrets of the night.
Silhouettes dance through the fading mist,
Each step taken, a chance not to miss.

Moonlit trails weave through ancient trees,
Guiding lost souls on a gentle breeze.
Stars twinkle softly, like forgotten dreams,
Leading us onward with its silver beams.

In shadows' depths, our fears take flight,
Facing the darkness, igniting the light.
Voices unspoken echo in our hearts,
Revealing the beauty in all of its parts.

These paths unseen, a journey we share,
Bound by the magic that hangs in the air.
With every heartbeat, adventure begins,
On invisible paths, our spirit spins.

Chronicles of the Unexplored

Winds of adventure beckon us near,
To places untouched, beyond hope, beyond fear.
Maps of the heart lead us to the coast,
Where the waves sing a tune, we adore the most.

Mountains rise high, shrouded in mist,
Over valleys of treasure, waiting to be kissed.
Footprints of dreamers trace tales unknown,
In lands uncharted, our seeds are sown.

Rivers of wonder flow through the night,
Guiding our dreams with their shimmering light.
In every silence, a story unfolds,
Of lands yet to see and legends retold.

These chronicles wait for souls brave and bold,
With wisdom in journeys, more precious than gold.
In the heart of the unexplored we find,
The whispers of freedom that dance in the mind.

Breathing in the Unknown

Every dawn breaks with a sigh so deep,
Awakening dreams that dare not sleep.
In the chill of the morning, hope intertwines,
With the essence of life that forever shines.

Clouds drift softly through the brightening sky,
A canvas of colors, the day starts to fly.
In the labyrinth of hearts, shadows reside,
Embracing the unknown, we stand side by side.

Each whispered promise, a breath of belief,
Navigating moments that lead to relief.
Hands held tightly in the storm's gentle blow,
Finding the courage to breathe in the unknown.

As night falls slowly and stars start to rise,
We gather our dreams, like fireflies.
In the quiet whispers, we learn to forgive,
Breathing in the unknown, embracing to live.

Unseen Threads of Fate

In a tapestry woven by hands unseen,
The choices we make, like whispers, convene.
A thread pulled tight, a knot that won't break,
We dance on the edge of the paths they partake.

Stars above guide with their shimmering light,
Destinies crisscross in the fabric of night.
Moments like shadows, they flicker and fade,
Yet in every heartbeat, a promise is made.

The Distant Call of Adventure

Across the hills, where the wild winds blow,
A siren's song whispers, urging to go.
Footsteps on pathways that twist and turn,
In the heart of the wanderer, a fire to burn.

Mountains loom high, with secrets untold,
Oceans stretch wide, beckoning bold.
Each corner a canvas, each mile a new tale,
Drifting like leaves in the soft summer gale.

Glimmers of the Unfamiliar

In the shadowed corners where dreams intertwine,
Flickers of magic in places divine.
Eyes wide with wonder at sights never seen,
Moments alive with a mystic sheen.

A garden of whispers stirs deep in the night,
Stars dance like fireflies, igniting the light.
Feel the pulse of the world, let it guide you there,
To realms where the heart learns to breathe in the rare.

The Language of Shadows

In the twilight hours, where secrets reside,
Shadows converse with the moon as their guide.
They speak in silence, yet echo so clear,
A cryptic ballet that only few hear.

Flickering edges, stories take flight,
A whisper of darkness, a hint of the light.
In the space between breaths, life's mysteries grow,
The language of shadows, forever in flow.

Secrets Woven in Silence

In shadows deep where whispers dwell,
The stories hide, they weave and swell.
Amidst the hush, where secrets cling,
A tapestry of dreams takes wing.

Voices muted, thoughts entwined,
In quiet corners, truth is blind.
The heart holds close what lips won't speak,
In silence bold, the soul feels weak.

Yet in the dark, a spark ignites,
The courage born from hidden fights.
Each breath a key to worlds unknown,
In whispered moments, we have grown.

Where No Footprints Lie

Beyond the dunes where echoes fade,
The sands remember, unafraid.
Here time stands still, no paths to trace,
A canvas bare, a tranquil space.

Beneath the stars, we find our way,
In silence deep, come what may.
With every step, we leave behind,
The weight of world, the ties that bind.

Nature cheers as wild hearts roam,
In fields of green, we build our home.
Where no footprints lie, we soar and glide,
In endless skies where dreams abide.

The Breath of What Lies Beyond

In twilight's glow, the whispers call,
The secrets held in nature's thrall.
Each sigh of wind, a promise made,
Of hopes that linger in the shade.

With every breath, we seek to find,
The mysteries woven in the blind.
A world unfolding, vast and free,
The breath of what we yearn to see.

From mountains high to oceans wide,
We chase the thoughts our hearts confide.
In every heartbeat, life's refrain,
Awakens all that we contain.

Cartography of Forgotten Places

Upon the map of lost domains,
Lie stories etched in ancient stains.
Forgotten paths and dreams long gone,
In faded ink, they linger on.

The mountains rise, the valleys dip,
In every line, a whispered trip.
Echoes of lives left behind,
In every curve, a tale aligned.

Through tangled woods, we wander still,
In search of echoes that time cannot kill.
The heart beats loud where silence lays,
In cartography of forgotten ways.

The Palette of Unwelcome Thoughts

Shadows creep where silence falls,
Brush strokes of doubt on empty walls.
Whispers dance in a restless mind,
Colors of fear that are cruelly designed.

A canvas stained by secret fears,
Drips of ink that resemble tears.
The weight of thoughts, a heavy hand,
In the gallery of a barren land.

Brush aside the shades of gray,
Paint a sunrise that leads the way.
Yet here I stand, caught in the fight,
With every stroke, I search for light.

In the depths of this painted night,
Emerging truths begin to ignite.
A palette old, but one that can heal,
Sketching dreams, lost hopes reveal.

Echoes of the Uncharted Universe

Beyond the stars, where silence reigns,
Whispers of worlds exist in chains.
Galaxies spin in a cosmic waltz,
Echoes of time, without a fault.

In the vastness, shadows blend,
Mysteries that twist and bend.
Each star a story, lost in years,
Dancing in silence, hidden tears.

Light years travel in briefest moments,
Unseen realms hold untold torments.
Beyond the known, the brave can go,
Chasing whispers of the unknown flow.

Yet in this space, we find a spark,
A trace of warmth in the endless dark.
Connected hearts, under one sky,
In uncharted realms, we learn to fly.

Illuminations of Dusty Tomorrows

Dusty roads where shadows lie,
Faded hopes that once soared high.
In corners where dreams gather dust,
Time's embrace, a silent trust.

Illuminations flicker bright,
Guiding paths through the night.
Each step forward, a tale to tell,
In whispered breaths, our wishes swell.

Yet heavy hangs the weight of yesterdays,
Clutching tight in unseen ways.
But glimmers break through tormented past,
In moments bright, we find peace at last.

Tomorrow waits in soft embrace,
Ready to dawn with gentle grace.
Dust may settle, but hearts will learn,
In every twilight, hopes will burn.

The Realm Beyond Perception

Beyond the veil where visions blur,
Lies a realm where thoughts concur.
A tapestry woven in silent threads,
Where whispers of the unseen spreads.

In shadows cast by light's embrace,
Secrets linger in timeless space.
Unfolding layers we cannot see,
Mysteries dance, wild and free.

Not bound by limits of earthly minds,
This realm is where true magic finds.
Each heartbeat echoes with a song,
Guiding travelers to where they belong.

In this space, perception bends,
Beginning of journeys, where light transcends.
Open the door, let wonder ignite,
For beyond the known, awaits the night.

Landscapes Beyond the Familiar

Mountains rise like ancient kings,
Veils of mist their secret brings.
Rivers weave through emerald lands,
Nature's brush, with gentle hands.

Skies ablaze in sunset's fire,
Whispers of the wild conspire.
Fields of gold where shadows play,
Echoes of the close of day.

Paths unseen invite the bold,
Stories waiting to be told.
In this realm where dreams are spun,
Journey starts with setting sun.

Wonders bloom in every nook,
Pages turn in nature's book.
Beyond the known, the heart shall leap,
In landscapes vast, our spirits steep.

Journeys into the Uncharted

Mapless roads stretch far and wide,
Adventurers seek their guide.
Through the fog, horizons gleam,
In the night, we chase a dream.

Footprints fade on shifting sands,
Every step, a tale expands.
With the dawn, new visions wake,
In the silence, paths we make.

Whispers fan the fires of hope,
In the dark, we learn to cope.
Into the wild, our spirits soar,
Every heartbeat calls for more.

With the stars as our design,
Every journey shall entwine.
Into the depths where wonders gleam,
We find ourselves, we find our dream.

Portals to the Unimagined

Windows open wide to skies,
Colors dance, the spirit flies.
In a world where time stands still,
Imagination bends our will.

Shapes and forms begin to blur,
Mysteries arise, hearts stir.
Every corner holds a tale,
In the breeze, our dreams set sail.

Through the shadows, visions roam,
In the silence, we find home.
Whispers echo through the night,
Guiding dreams to take their flight.

Cycles twist in vibrant hues,
Boundless paths, we choose to view.
Portals to the worlds unseen,
In our hearts, the light shall glean.

Secrets Lurking Beneath

Silent waters, deep and wide,
Hidden truths that nature hides.
Underneath the surface glow,
Patterns drift, a tale in flow.

Roots entangle in the earth,
Whispers share of life and birth.
Beneath the bark, a story breathes,
All is woven, none deceives.

In the shadows of the tall,
Voices echo, rise and fall.
Secrets linger, waiting still,
To unfold with gentle will.

In the depths, a treasure gleams,
Anchored in our silent dreams.
Secrets whispered through the years,
Teach us laughter, teach us tears.

Secrets Beneath the Surface

Whispers soft in shadowed halls,
Beneath the waves, the silence calls.
Hidden tales and veiled desires,
Buried deep where truth conspires.

Glimmers dance in murky depths,
Ancient echoes of lost breaths.
Secrets wrapped in ocean's sway,
Waiting for the light of day.

Fingers trace the sandy floor,
Every grain has known before.
Veins of stories intertwine,
In the dark, the secrets shine.

Beneath the calm, the tempest brews,
The heart holds all, yet fears to choose.
In silence, hidden gems reside,
Waiting for the world to guide.

The Uncharted Pathways

Winding trails through forests dense,
Every step, a consequence.
Footprints lost to time and fate,
Destinies that lie in wait.

Mist clings low as dawn unfolds,
Each direction, untold golds.
Every twist, a chance unspun,
Journey starts with just one run.

Maps and signs may lead astray,
Yet the heart knows where to sway.
Along these paths, the wilds call,
A beckoning within us all.

In the shade of ancient trees,
Dreams take flight upon the breeze.
With courage as our guiding star,
We'll find the way, no matter how far.

Dreams of the Forgotten Realm

In realms where shadow gently plays,
Whispers weave through silver haze.
Lost in time, the echoes swell,
As ancient stories weave their spell.

Hidden realms of dusk and dawn,
Where the lost and loved are drawn.
In the silence, memories flow,
Painting worlds we long to know.

Fables told by starlit streams,
Crown our nights and fill our dreams.
In that place, our hearts reside,
Awakening where dreams abide.

Through the mist, familiarity grows,
Embracing all that time bestows.
In that realm, we'll always meet,
Where imagination finds its seat.

Lurking in the Twilight

As daylight fades and shadows creep,
Secrets stir from quiet sleep.
Figures dance in fading light,
As the world prepares for night.

In the gloam, the mystery reigns,
Whispers echo through the plains.
All that glitters starts to fade,
Lost beneath the twilight's shade.

Every sound a haunting call,
In the darkness, we stand tall.
Chasing dreams that ebb and flow,
While the stars begin to glow.

In this hour of dusk's embrace,
We find strength in the unknown space.
Together, we shall face the dark,
For there's magic in every spark.

Fragments of a Hidden Narrative

Whispers in the shadows play,
Secrets unfold in disarray.
Time holds tight to tales untold,
Fragments of life, both faint and bold.

Stories trapped in twilight's glow,
Memories bend and twist like flow.
Each glimpse a treasure, a fleeting light,
Fragments dance in the depths of night.

Words like echoes in a dream,
Beneath the surface, a silent scream.
In every corner, a tale resides,
Fragments of truth that fate provides.

Life's canvas painted in shades of gray,
Hidden narratives that guide the way.
In every heart, a story's beat,
Fragments of life, incomplete yet sweet.

Portals to the Unexplored

Through the veil where shadows stride,
Open portals where secrets hide.
Curious minds seek paths unknown,
To unexplored realms, a journey flown.

Winds of change whisper 'come near',
Inviting souls to abandon fear.
Every step, a new world reflects,
Portals to wonder, what life expects.

Starlit skies call out in grace,
A dance of dreams in time and space.
Every heartbeat, a story shared,
Portals of hope, we are all dared.

With every dawn, new chances breathe,
Adventures waiting, just believe.
Through the portals where hearts connect,
The unexplored paths we seek to trek.

The Enigma of What Lies Ahead

Paths diverge in tangled woods,
An enigma lingers where fortune broods.
Footprints vanish, paths unfold,
The future whispers secrets bold.

In the distance, dreams ignite,
Floating hopes in the dead of night.
Each choice we make, a silent thread,
Woven stories of what lies ahead.

Questions linger like morning dew,
The unknown dances in shades of blue.
Yet within the chaos, a promise stands,
The enigma guided by unseen hands.

Embrace the journey, let fears subside,
In the face of doubt, let courage guide.
For what lies ahead, in shadows or flood,
Is shaped by the dreams that we have begun.

Mysteries in the Mist

Veils of gray drape the land,
Mysteries hidden, yet close at hand.
Every step through the quiet air,
Brings whispers of tales, a silent flair.

The fog enfolds each whispered tune,
Beneath the stars, beneath the moon.
Lost in shadows, secrets blend,
Mysteries waiting, hearts to mend.

Shapes emerge from the velvet haze,
Glimmers of truth in the labyrinth's maze.
Each breath a moment, rich and crisp,
In the mist, gentle mysteries wisp.

Curiosity ignites the soul,
In the unknown, we seek to be whole.
For in the mist, life holds its might,
Mysteries unfurl, igniting the night.

Within the Labyrinth of Dreams

In shadows deep, where whispers dwell,
Veils of night cast their mystic spell.
Each step a dance on paths unseen,
Where moonlight weaves through dreams serene.

Fragments flicker, like stars in flight,
Guiding the wanderer through the night.
Echoes of laughter, soft and low,
In the labyrinth, all secrets flow.

Winding corridors of hope and fear,
Each turn a sigh, each breath a tear.
Lost in the maze of what could be,
The heart searches for its memory.

Awake or asleep, what is the line?
In the realm of dreams, all things align.
Through tangled paths, I'll find my way,
In the labyrinth where my dreams play.

Gazing into the Abyss

A chasm calls with a voice so clear,
Whispers of truth, both far and near.
In depths unknown, shadows entwine,
What lies beneath, a shifting sign.

Echoes of silence, a haunting song,
In the abyss, where lost souls belong.
Gaze into darkness, confront the fear,
In the void, what do we hold dear?

Eyes like the stars, they flicker fast,
In the depths where memories last.
What horrors dwell in the stillness there?
What dreams awaken in the midnight air?

Yet in this darkness, a glimmer ignites,
A flicker of hope, through the endless nights.
Gazing deeply, a truth emerges,
From the abyss, our soul converges.

Tales Untold by Time

Whispers of ages, woven tight,
Stories long lost drift into sight.
Time's gentle hand can't erase the past,
In silences kept, our shadows cast.

Echoes of laughter, echoes of tears,
In pages turned, the weight of years.
Glimpses of life in fragments reside,
Tales untold where memories bide.

The clock runs on, yet still we wait,
For threads of fate to intertwine and create.
Stories buried in the sands of time,
Unspooled by fate, through rhythm and rhyme.

In every heartbeat, a story unfolds,
In each fleeting moment, a truth enfolds.
Tales untold, yearning to sing,
In the silence, their echoes take wing.

Beyond the Boundaries of Belief

In realms uncharted, where visions collide,
Beyond the limits we dare to abide.
Thoughts like rivers flow wild and free,
Breaking the chains of what we can see.

A spark of wonder ignites the air,
Inviting the dreamers to venture and dare.
What lies beyond, in the great unknown?
In the heart's whispers, true courage is sown.

To reach for the stars, to taste the sky,
With every question, we learn to fly.
In the spaces where doubts find release,
We find ourselves in a sense of peace.

Boundaries fade when the heart believes,
In the magic of hopes, the spirit weaves.
Beyond the borders where dreams take flight,
In the land of belief, all things unite.

Veils of the Unseen

In twilight's shroud, secrets hide,
Mysteries dance on the edge of night.
A flicker here, a shadow there,
What lies beneath, forever out of sight.

Glimmers of truth, like grains of sand,
Slip through fingers of the restless hand.
In whispers soft, the veils will sway,
Revealing worlds often led astray.

Moonlit paths, where shadows creep,
Echoes of dreams, in silence seep.
Yet through the haze, a light might break,
A glimpse of hope for the lost to take.

Veils entwined in fateful lore,
Each thread a tale, of forevermore.
Through unseen hands, we are all bound,
In the stillness, our hearts resound.

Whispers Beyond the Horizon

In dawn's embrace, whispers rise,
Soft winds carry tales from the skies.
Beyond the waves, where sea meets land,
Secrets of time stretch hand in hand.

Through golden fields and silver streams,
Nature hums ancient, untold dreams.
Each rustling leaf, a story spun,
In the silence, life has begun.

Mountains stand Majestic and tall,
Holding secrets within their call.
A journey beckons, beckons anew,
To wander where the wild hearts flew.

So chase the horizon, embrace the light,
In every shadow, find your flight.
For whispers linger, close yet far,
Guiding the soul, like a vibrant star.

In the Shadows of Silence

In shadows deep, where silence reigns,
Whispers of thoughts slip through the chains.
An echo soft, a heartbeat faint,
In muted realms where colors paint.

Beneath the surface, feelings stir,
In quiet moments, souls concur.
A breath, a sigh, a fleeting thought,
In stillness, battles are silently fought.

Yet in this hush, a power resides,
A sanctuary where truth abides.
For in the pause, we often find,
The deepest echoes of the mind.

So venture forth into the shade,
Where silence speaks, and fears invade.
In shadows' dance, let wisdom unfurl,
In the hush of night, discover your world.

Echoes from the Abyss

From the depths of dark, a call resounds,
Echoes of souls lost, yet still they surround.
In the silence thick, their stories blend,
Through time and space, they twist and bend.

Whispers of sorrow, of joy once bright,
Resonate softly through the endless night.
Each flicker of hope, a star in the void,
A tapestry woven, never destroyed.

Deep in the dark, secrets unwind,
In the heart of the abyss, what truths we find.
The past can linger like shadows cast,
Yet forward we tread, free from the past.

So listen close, as the echoes call,
In the abyss, we rise or fall.
For in the depths, a spark may gleam,
Guiding the lost toward the dream.

Threads of the Unfamiliar

In shadows deep where whispers dance,
A tapestry of chance and trance.
Unraveled dreams thread through the night,
Binding paths in soft moonlight.

With every stitch a story spun,
In silence where the heartbeats run.
The fabric weaves a strange delight,
Unfamiliar souls take flight.

Colors blend, emotions sway,
In tangled knots, we lose our way.
Yet through the dark a glimpse we find,
Of threads connecting heart and mind.

So let us wander on this road,
In the depths of the unknown code.
For therein lies the sacred art,
Of threads that weave the human heart.

The Echo of an Unsung Journey

A step into the silent dawn,
Where echoes of the lost are drawn.
Each footfall marks a shadowed path,
Unveiling tales that time forgot.

Through valleys deep and mountains high,
The whispers of the past still sigh.
For every story left untold,
Lives in the echoes, fierce and bold.

With every echo sings the heart,
Of journeys where the soul takes part.
Each stumble leads to brighter skies,
A dance of dreams where spirit flies.

Let the chorus of the brave ring clear,
For in their song, no fear draws near.
An unsung journey waits ahead,
In echoes where the heart is fed.

In Search of the Unfathomable

Beyond the stars, where thoughts collide,
We seek the truth that time won't hide.
In depths of dark, the light remains,
A quest to break the unseen chains.

In shadows stretched by endless night,
We search for sparks of hidden light.
Every tear a wave, every sigh,
In vast unknown, we yearn and cry.

With every heartbeat, questions grow,
In search of peace, we ebb and flow.
The unfathomable calls our name,
In whispers soft, igniting flame.

And though the path is steep and long,
We dance with doubts, we craft our song.
For in this search, we find our place,
In the unfathomable, we embrace.

Colors Beyond the Known Spectrum

In the realm where colors blend,
Beyond the sight, where visions mend.
A palette rich with shades untold,
Awakens dreams in hues of gold.

Each brushstroke, a whisper bright,
Painting worlds of pure delight.
From violets deep to crimson's fire,
In colors born from heart's desire.

Beyond the known, where spirits soar,
Textures change and spirits pour.
For every shade a story weaves,
In colors caught in autumn leaves.

So let us roam this vibrant place,
In every hue, the heart's embrace.
For in the colors that we find,
Lies the infinite in the mind.

Secrets Beneath the Surface

Beneath the waves, a world concealed,
Echoes of stories, long revealed.
Silent whispers in the deep blue,
Secrets hidden, waiting for you.

Ancient ruins, lost in the sand,
Memories linger, a ghostly hand.
Sunken treasures, tales of old,
In depths of silence, secrets unfold.

With every ripple, a hint of fate,
Life intertwines, it's never too late.
Bubbles rise, like thoughts to share,
Beneath the surface, dreams lay bare.

Dive into darkness, explore and see,
What lies beneath, sets the spirit free.
In hidden depths, adventure calls,
Secrets awaken as the ocean falls.

The Veil of Mysteries

In twilight hours, the shadows dance,
Veils of secrets, a fleeting chance.
Whispers linger, wrapped in night,
Mysteries twinkle, lost in light.

Pages turned in ancient books,
Hidden truths in overlooked nooks.
Every glance a puzzle, untold,
The veil shrouds what's pure and bold.

Echoes resound through silent halls,
Ghostly figures in faded walls.
A dance of visions, blurred and clear,
The veil of mysteries draws us near.

Beneath the surface of what we see,
Lies a realm of possibilities free.
Each thread woven in time's embrace,
The veil hides wonders, a sacred space.

Shadows of Unexplored Realms

Beyond the known, where shadows creep,
Uncharted paths, a timeless leap.
In twilight's grasp, secrets reside,
Unexplored realms, where dreams collide.

Echoing steps on ancient stone,
Mysteries whisper, never alone.
In the dark, a flicker ignites,
Shadows dance in the heart of night.

Caves of wonder, rich and deep,
Harvest the thoughts that silence keeps.
Every corner, a story to tell,
In shadows' embrace, we weave our spells.

In the stillness, a quiet call,
The allure of shadows beckons us all.
Venturing forth, with courage to dare,
To explore the realms that linger in air.

Whispers Across the Abyss

Across the void, the echoes flow,
Whispers carry where few dare go.
In the silence, truths interweave,
A tapestry of what we believe.

Blackened waters, depth unknown,
With shadows dancing, seeds are sown.
Each flicker of light, a distant guide,
Whispers across the endless tide.

Yearning hearts in twilight's grace,
Seeking solace in this strange place.
In the abyss, hope still ignites,
Carried by whispers of starry nights.

To reach beyond what we can see,
Is to embrace our destiny.
Across the abyss, where dreams take flight,
Whispers lead us into the night.

Reflections in the Dark

Whispers of night, shadows draw near,
Echoes of thoughts, crystal and clear.
In the stillness, secrets take flight,
Dreams linger soft in the heart of the night.

Moonlit paths, a silvery gleam,
Tracing the edges of every dream.
Silent confessions, a gentle embark,
Painted in whispers, reflections in dark.

Fleeting glances, mysteries unfold,
Tales woven softly, waiting to be told.
In the deep quiet, we find our embrace,
Basking in shadows, lost in time's trace.

As the dawn breaks, colors ignite,
Carrying whispers from darkness to light.
Reflections may fade, but the essence will spark,
Inside our hearts, we'll cherish the dark.

Legends of the Untold

Beneath the mountains, in valleys so wide,
Whispers of legends, where secrets abide.
Echoes of battles, of courage unbowed,
In the silence of nature, a brave heart is proud.

Ancient stones cradle tales from the past,
Woven with dreams, binding shadows steadfast.
From fires long extinguished, a warmth still survives,
Each tale a reminder, our spirit still thrives.

Wonders of ages, entwined in the breeze,
Forgotten stories that rustle the leaves.
Through mist and through twilight, we seek and behold,
The magic that lingers in legends untold.

With every heartbeat, history calls,
Echoing softly through silent stone halls.
In the depths of our souls, we cherish and hold,
The power of stories, the legends of old.

Starlight on Secret Waters

Glistening ripples, beneath the night sky,
Whispers of starlight, as time drifts by.
Moonbeams caress the surface so bright,
A dance of reflections, a mystical sight.

Hidden horizons where dreams gently flow,
Secrets of waters that shimmer and glow.
In the silence, tranquility sings,
Embracing the night with the joy that it brings.

Gently we linger on the edge of the deep,
Lost in the beauty where silence will keep.
Each moment a treasure, a memory to hold,
Starlight on waters, pure magic unfolds.

As dawn approaches, the stars bid farewell,
In the heart of the night, their stories do dwell.
Forever imprinted, in whispers they stay,
On secret waters, where dreams find their way.

Footsteps in the Unfamiliar

Wandering forth on paths unexplored,
Each step a question, the heart's true reward.
In gardens of twilight, mysteries grow,
Footprints of wanderers, long lost to the flow.

Voices of strangers, each face a tale,
In the dance of the unknown, we drift like a sail.
Moments that shimmer like dewdrops in light,
Guiding our spirits through the velvet of night.

With courage we forge, through shadows we'll tread,
Finding the wisdom in words left unsaid.
The map of our journey, inked with regret,
Footsteps of growth, the paths we won't forget.

Every intersection, a world to embrace,
In the tapestry of life, we find our place.
Through the unfamiliar, we learn to believe,
With each footstep taken, new dreams we conceive.

The Light in Uncharted Waters

In depths where silence dwells, it glows,
A beacon bright, its warmth bestows.
Waves whisper tales of untold years,
Guiding lost souls through hidden fears.

The night is vast, yet hope ignites,
With every wave, new dreams take flight.
Riding currents strong and free,
The light invites discovery.

Among the shadows, secrets hide,
Yet courage swells, a rising tide.
For every heart that dares to tread,
The light reveals what lies ahead.

Through treacherous paths and stormy skies,
It shines through, breaking darkened ties.
In uncharted waters, life may spring,
From depths of doubt, a vibrant thing.

Where Dreams Daunt

In corners dark, where shadows creep,
Ambitions fade, like whispers deep.
Yet hearts still linger, grasping time,
To face the fears that oh so climb.

Each step a challenge, doubts entwined,
But strength lies dormant in the mind.
A spark ignites within the night,
A flicker bold, a chance to fight.

Where dreams may daunt and tales grow thin,
Resilience whispers, 'You can win.'
With every fall, a lesson learned,
The fire within will never burn.

In the vast expanse of silent cries,
Hope weaves through darkened skies.
A journey long, yet worth the strife,
For on the other side is life.

Through the Fabric of Shadows

In whispers soft, the shadows weave,
Tales of light, and those who grieve.
Through fabric thick, a story spins,
Of dreams unclaimed and silent sins.

Each thread a heart, a memory shared,
In patterns complex, emotions bared.
Yet from the gloom, a shimmer fights,
A quest for truth, igniting nights.

Through tangled threads, we seek to find,
The courage to leave fears behind.
For shadows dance in fleeting grace,
Revealing paths we must embrace.

In twilight's grasp, the journey calls,
Echoing softly through hallowed halls.
Through the fabric, we'll forge our way,
To brighter dawns, and hopeful days.

The Anatomy of Hidden Lives

Beneath the surface, stories lie,
Anatomy of dreams that never die.
Hidden lives with secrets swell,
In silent echoes, they softly dwell.

In whispered thoughts, the truth conceals,
A tapestry of hope that heals.
Each life a thread in world's expanse,
Yearning for light, a fleeting chance.

With every heartbeat, tales unfold,
In shades of grey, in blue and gold.
Unraveled layers of joy and pain,
In hidden lives, sunshine and rain.

The anatomy of souls revealed,
Through every scar, a heart healed.
For in the shadows, beauty twines,
In the hidden, the divine shines.

The Edge of Familiarity

In shadows cast by whispered fears,
We linger close, yet far apart.
The echoes hold our laughter, tears,
A gentle nudge within the heart.

Each step we take, a measured dance,
Upon the brink of what we know.
Familiar paths, yet in a trance,
We seek the light, a softer glow.

The sun may rise, the stars may fall,
In moments fleeting, bold, or shy.
Yet here we stand, despite it all,
At edge of dreams that ever fly.

We crave the known and yearn for change,
A paradox that stirs the soul.
Embracing both, we rearrange,
A tapestry that makes us whole.

Illusions of the Lost

In twilight's grasp, the shadows blend,
A haunting song of those long gone.
We chase the echoes, seek to mend,
The broken threads of ages drawn.

With every sigh, a ghostly spark,
Illusions dance in fading light.
We wander through the endless dark,
In search of meaning, hope, and sight.

Yet what is lost may still remain,
In memories that softly call.
A phantom touch, a bittersweet pain,
The past, our guide through it all.

So let us walk this wooded trail,
Where every leaf tells tales untold.
In fragile dreams, we'll never fail,
To find the warmth in memories bold.

Inhabiting the Invisible

Beyond the veil where silence dwells,
We trace the lines of what we feel.
Each breath a secret, stories tell,
Of worlds unseen, yet so surreal.

In shadows deep, we often roam,
Inhabiting the space between.
A whispered thought may find a home,
Where light and dark convene, serene.

The whispers swell within our minds,
A tapestry of shade and light.
Invisible ties that fate designed,
Unravel in the quiet night.

So let us dwell where thoughts expand,
In realms of dreams where hopes align.
To touch the void with open hands,
In the unseen, our souls entwine.

Beyond the Known Veil

In twilight's hue, we find our way,
Through territories unexplored.
With cautious hearts, we dare to stray,
To seek the truths we've long ignored.

The stars above our guiding light,
Illuminate the paths ahead.
In shadows deep, we face the night,
And venture forth where few have tread.

Beyond the known, the brave reside,
With courage stitched in every seam.
For in the dark, we learn to glide,
And weave our destinies, it seems.

So hold my hand, we'll leap with grace,
Into the wild, the vast unknown.
Together, we'll embrace the space,
Beyond the veil where dreams have grown.

Navigating the Impenetrable

In a maze of whispers, I tread soft,
Each corner hides secrets, dreams held aloft.
With shadows as guides, I seek the way,
Through veils of uncertainty, night turns to day.

Silent echoes call, I follow their lead,
To the heart of the chaos, where fears must concede.
Each step taken brings a pulse of the night,
In the depths of the dark, I find a new light.

Paths intertwine like the threads of a loom,
Creating a tapestry, stitching the gloom.
With courage as armor, I face every wall,
In this dance with the unknown, I shall not fall.

Navigating through turmoil, I rise and I bend,
In the labyrinth of life, I discover a friend.
Through the impassable, I carve out my space,
In the beauty of struggle, I find my own grace.

Fragments of Unfathomable Experiences

Whispers of moments slip through my hands,
Like grains of sand swept across distant lands.
Each shard holds a story, a glimpse, a truth,
Fragments scattered widely, remnants of youth.

In shadows of memory, colors collide,
Emotions resurface, no place to hide.
Lost in the echoes, I search for the whole,
As pieces connect, they reveal my soul.

The fabric of time, stitched with care,
Every thread tells of love, longing, and despair.
In the cacophony, clarity shines,
Fragments unite, and my spirit aligns.

With each revelation, I dance with the past,
Embracing the lessons, I hold them steadfast.
These fragments are guideposts, like stars in the night,
Leading me forward, wrapped in their light.

Dreams in a Strangely Colored Light

In twilight's embrace, vivid dreams unfurl,
Painted in hues of an enigmatic world.
Each brushstroke whispers tales of the mind,
In this strangely colored light, peace I find.

Floating on clouds of cerulean grace,
Timeless adventures in this surreal space.
The ordinary dims, as fantasies soar,
In the glow of creation, I yearn for more.

Silhouettes dance under a lavender sky,
Every heartbeat echoes, a jubilant sigh.
In the warmth of the glow, fears gently fade,
Dreams weave a tapestry, intricately laid.

Awake in the canvas, I redefine fate,
Every color a chance, every shape creates.
In this living mosaic, I lose track of time,
Beneath strangely colored light, life's rhythm is rhyme.

Shadows Cast on Unfamiliar Ground

In the dusk of twilight, shadows begin,
Stretching like secrets, thin whispers within.
Each step on this path is a story untold,
In the guise of the night, new truths unfold.

Ghostly figures beckon, familiar yet strange,
Lost in their presence, I sense the exchange.
With every soft footfall on this unknown earth,
I embrace the enigma, the chance for rebirth.

Flickers of memory, like stars in the dark,
Guide me through silence, a spiritual spark.
Through the shadows I wander, discovering grace,
In the haunting of stillness, I find my place.

Each shadow a mirror, reflecting my soul,
Through unfamiliar ground, I become whole.
With courage as compass, I journey profound,
In the shadows of night, there's beauty unbound.

In the Wake of Unraveled Whispers

In shadows cast by twilight's hand,
Whispers linger, soft and grand.
They weave through dreams like threads of gold,
Stories of secrets quietly told.

Each sigh a breeze, each breath a sigh,
Floating gently, like a lullaby.
In the wake, the echoes blend,
A tapestry of thoughts to send.

With every murmur, a tale unfolds,
Hints of truths and fables bold.
In silence, a world starts to sing,
And hidden wonders begin to spring.

As night descends, the whispers grow,
An orchestra of the unseen flow.
In twilight's grasp, we find our place,
Embracing words that time won't chase.

The Story Behind Closed Eyes

Behind closed eyes, a universe lies,
Where dreams take flight and never die.
Colors swirling, shadows dance,
Moments captured in a trance.

Silent echoes of laughter ring,
In this realm, the heart takes wing.
Stories woven in fabric of night,
A tapestry spun with pure delight.

From distant lands, the tales arrive,
Carried softly, like a whispered jive.
Ancient voices call from afar,
Guiding seekers to their star.

What lies within, the heart knows best,
In dreams, we find our truest quest.
Behind closed eyes, the world is wide,
A secret haven where we reside.

Structures of the Unaccounted

Forgotten walls tell tales of strife,
Structures bearing the weight of life.
Each crack a memory, each stone a sigh,
History whispers as moments fly.

Lost in the ruins of what once was,
Echoes of laughter, love's quiet buzz.
Among the shadows, shadows meet,
Footsteps linger, discreet and sweet.

Brick by brick, foundations laid,
In the silence, a promise made.
The stories dwell in cracks so deep,
Guardians hold what we must keep.

In the architecture of the unseen,
Lies the heart of what has been.
Structures rise as memories fade,
In the unaccounted, dreams are made.

Sounds from Faraway Lands

In the distance, songs arise,
Melodies carried through sapphire skies.
Whispers of winds from realms unknown,
A symphony of cultures, grown.

Notes of laughter, tones of grace,
Drift like shadows to a sacred place.
Beating drums echo through the night,
Stories woven in the pale moonlight.

From mountains high to valleys wide,
Songs of the heart, a vibrant tide.
With every breeze, a different tale,
Colors of language in every scale.

Each sound a bridge to lands afar,
Uniting souls like a guiding star.
In the chorus of life, we find our song,
Together as one, we always belong.

Whispers of the Unimagined

In shadows where the dreams reside,
A soft breeze carries tales untold,
Colors dance beyond our sight,
Whispers weave through thoughts of old.

What lies beyond the waking mind?
A realm where visions intertwine,
Infinite creatures, wild and free,
With echoes of a world divine.

In the silence, secrets bloom,
Crafting worlds of wonder near,
Voices rise from quiet gloom,
Drawing every heart to hear.

Take a step, let go of fear,
Embrace the dreams that softly call,
For in the unimagined, dear,
We find ourselves, we find it all.

The Forgotten Echo

In the stillness of the night,
A whisper fades into the dark,
Memories drift, a haunting flight,
Leaving only shadows stark.

Amidst the ruins of the past,
Voices linger, soft and low,
Stories woven, fading fast,
Yet in the heart, a flicker glows.

Timeless echoes call our name,
Reminding us of what has been,
In every silence, there's a flame,
The forgotten lives we've seen.

To feel the pulse of bygone days,
Is to embrace the lost and found,
In each echo, love still plays,
In every silence, life resounds.

Treading on Unfamiliar Soil

With every step, a heartbeat thrums,
The ground beneath, alive with change,
Paths unknown, where wonder hums,
Familiar comforts soon feel strange.

Fields of green and skies so wide,
Each journey brings a brand-new view,
In fresh encounters, fears subside,
New stories greet all who pursue.

In this place of twilight gleam,
Hopes awaken like the dawn,
Dreams emerge from every seam,
In the soil where fears are drawn.

To tread on paths we dare not tread,
Opens hearts to all that's new,
For every step foresakes the dread,
And leads us to the truest you.

Beyond the Boundaries of Knowing

In the void where questions swell,
Curiosity dares to soar,
Beyond our grasp, a hidden spell,
Awaits the truths we yearn for.

Uncharted seas and stars untamed,
Invite the brave to navigate,
In every quest, knowledge claimed,
Awakens worlds, unlocks the gate.

To seek the wonder in the night,
Is to embrace the vast unknown,
With every spark, a burst of light,
Beckoning hearts to claim their own.

So venture forth, let dreams unfold,
For in the chase, we find our song,
Through mysteries, our lives are told,
Beyond the realms, we all belong.

Milton Keynes UK
Ingram Content Group UK Ltd.
UKHW022006131124
451149UK00013B/1034